Lots [illegible] ut money and [illegible] when the topi [illegible] book that take [illegible] says about money and generosity. But it doesn't stop there. Des Smith is, at heart, a pastorso he insightfully lands what the Bible says to shape our motivations and practice. This is a very positive tool in a culture where love of money is a huge issue.

Paul Harrington
Senior Pastor, Trinity Network of Churches, Adelaide

I've had the privilege being involved in the production of a number of resources that encourage Christians to be generous and train gospel workers to raise support. It is a big topic. *The Cheerful Giver* is like the 'Blinklist' or 'Sparknotes' book that summarizes the Bible's teaching brilliantly. It has a beautifully simple structure. The first three (of four) chapters ask three key questions: "Why should we give?", "How much should we give?" and "Who should we give to?" Simple. *The Cheerful Giver* took me 65 minutes to read. How good is that? Jesus Christ's generosity is marvelled at throughout. The points made from Scripture are faithful and true. The illustrations are superb. And Des ends the book by explaining how he and his family organize their own financial giving.

As an aside, Des has done some stand-up comedy ... so the book is quite fun to read. And in it I learnt that God is "flahoolick". You'll have to buy the book to find out what that means!

I wholeheartedly commend *The Cheerful Giver.*

Ben Pfahlert
National Director, Ministry Training Strategy, Sydney

The Cheerful Giver

A short guide to gospel-driven giving

The Cheerful Giver

A short guide to gospel-driven giving

Des Smith

matthiasmedia
SYDNEY • YOUNGSTOWN

The Cheerful Giver

Matthias Media
(St Matthias Press Ltd ACN 067 558 365)
Email: info@matthiasmedia.com.au
Internet: matthiasmedia.com.au
Please visit our website for current postal and telephone contact information.

Matthias Media (USA)
Email: sales@matthiasmedia.com
Internet: matthiasmedia.com
Please visit our website for current postal and telephone contact information.

All websites cited in this book were accessed on 30 January 2024.

ISBN 978 1 922980 21 2

Cover design and typesetting by Lankshear Design.

For my mum

Contents

Introduction

My first lesson in generosity came from my mother.

I was about six or seven years old. We were in the supermarket, and I noticed that something we needed was on special. There were boxes and boxes of it, but my mum only took two. I said to her, "Mum, they're on special, why don't we take them all?"

"Because we need to leave some for the poor people", my mum said, and we moved on.

I'm sure Mum never thought about that interaction again, but it's stuck with me ever since. It was a simple expression of thoughtfulness for other people, especially those less well off. We couldn't take everything, even though that would have been better for us, because we needed to leave some for others. It was a wonderful lesson in generosity.

This short book is about generosity, and I hope it also offers some good lessons—not because *I* have something to teach you about the topic, but because *the Bible* has so much to say about living generous lives and being generous people. This book is about what the Bible says about giving, and especially how the Christian gospel—the good news of what God has done for us in Jesus—guides our giving. In other words, it's not just a book about giving; it's a book about *gospel-driven giving.*

Of course, it won't say everything about the topic—that would take a much longer book! But it offers a short overview of a topic that raises a lot of big questions. In particular, it will answer three key questions.

1. Why give?

As Christians, we know instinctively that we should give, but we're sometimes unclear about *why*. Is it because we'll get into trouble with God if we don't? Or because he'll give to us in return if we do? Or some other reason? *Why* should we give?

2. How much should we give?

Once we have the *why* of giving sorted, we need to work out *how much* we should give. There is a lot of debate in Christian circles about this. Some Christians believe firmly that we should give a 'tithe' (ten percent) or more, in line with certain Old Testament laws; others believe there is no fixed percentage, and it's just up to the individual believer. So which is it? How much should we give?

3. Who should we give to?

Then, once we know *why* we give and we've reached a conclusion on *how much* we should give, we still need to work out *who we should give to*. We live in a world of limited resources, and we only have so much money to give away. But the needs are practically endless. So how should we divide up our giving? Does the Bible list people or causes we should give to? And does it give us any guidance on how to prioritize them?

These are the three questions this book will answer. I hope you find it useful.

One small note before we start: this is not just a book about giving to church. As we'll see in chapter 3, giving to church is one thing we should do, but it's not the only giving Christians should do—not by a long shot. Rather, as we grasp the gospel more and more, we'll be moved to give to many things, and to enjoy doing so. That's what this book is about: cheerfully giving to all the things God calls us to give to, because we're gripped by the gospel, and because "God loves a cheerful giver" (2 Cor 9:7).

As Jesus said, "It is more blessed to give than to receive" (Acts 20:35). And he really meant it. Let's find out why.

1 | Why should we give?

Why should Christians give?
Because God has given to us.

There. There's your answer. If you're short on time, you can turn to the next chapter now.

No, not really. We need to flesh this out before it will make sense. Let's think more about God's generosity to us, and why this should make us generous people.

God gives us everything

You probably aren't very familiar with 1 Chronicles 29, but it's an ideal place to begin our thinking about generosity.

The context is that King David is raising money for the temple that his son, Solomon, is planning to build. It's vital that the temple be excellent because it's *God's* temple (v 1), but at this point Solomon is "young and inexperienced". So it's important that the whole nation get behind the project and chip in. And they do! After announcing that the government will provide all the building materials (v 2) and promising to give from his own funds (vv 3–5a), David cries out to the people: "Now, who is willing to consecrate themselves to the Lord today?" (v 5b). In other words, who is also willing to give to this project? And the leaders of the people respond with astounding generosity, promising to give lots of money and resources (vv 6–9). What's more, the people rejoice "at the willing response of their leaders, for they [have] given freely and wholeheartedly to the Lord" (v 9). They have not been compelled to give, but have chosen to do so as an act of generosity. David joins them in their rejoicing.

David then prays before the people, reflecting on how Israel can be so generous. What does he say? Is it because the people of Israel have worked hard for everything they have and they're willing to 'do God a favour' and give him some money? No! David recognizes that they can only be so generous because God has given them everything in the first place:

> "Yours, Lord, is the greatness and the power
> and the glory and the majesty and the
> splendour,
> for everything in heaven and earth is yours.

Yours, Lord, is the kingdom;
you are exalted as head over all.
Wealth and honour come from you;
you are the ruler of all things.
In your hands are strength and power
to exalt and give strength to all.
Now, our God, we give you thanks,
and praise your glorious name.

"But who am I, and who are my people, that we should be able to give as generously as this? Everything comes from you, and we have given you only what comes from your hand." (vv 11–14)

David knows that everything they have comes from God, therefore anything they give to God is already his.

It reminds me of Christmas when I was a kid. My parents gave me presents and, of course, I wanted to give them presents back. But I was too young to have any money. So how could I buy them anything? My parents came up with the solution: they gave me some money, and I bought them presents with it (and I'm sure our family was not the only one that came up with this solution).

Were my parents pleased when I gave them their presents? Of course. But were they any financially better off? Of course not. I'd merely given them what was already theirs. I'd taken their money and returned it in the form of gifts. My parents were, as the saying goes, 'sixpence none the richer'.[1]

It's the same with God. Everything Israel has comes from him. So when they give towards building a temple for him, they're not really giving him anything, because it all belongs to him anyway. God owns "every animal of the forest ... and the cattle on a thousand hills" (Ps 50:10). The only reason they can be generous is because God has first been generous to them.

We can easily assume we have the things we have just because of our hard work. We look at all the stuff we've accumulated—our houses, cars, holidays, educations, and everything else we have—and think we deserve them because we've worked for them. Now, I'm sure you've worked hard for what you have. And God's word says that hard work usually results in people getting good things. For example, the Proverbs tell us: "All hard work brings a profit, but mere talk leads only to poverty" (Prov 14:23). Yet we don't *ultimately* have things because we work for them. Ultimately, we have

1 The expression seems to come from CS Lewis's book *Mere Christianity* (HarperCollins, 2016, p 143): "When we talk of a man doing anything for God or giving anything to God, I will tell you what it is really like. It is like a small child going to its father and saying, 'Daddy, give me sixpence to buy you a birthday present.' Of course, the father does, and he is pleased with the child's present. It is all very nice and proper, but only an idiot would think that the father is sixpence to the good on the transaction."

things because God gives them to us. The stone that forms the walls of my house, the steel and rubber in my car, the holiday destinations I enjoy—God made them all, and they existed well before I did.

"Sure", you may say, "but my hard work meant that I could get them". But even your hard work—your capacity to work, the breath in your lungs, the blood in your veins, the electrons whizzing around in your brain—all came from God. You don't draw breath without God's say-so, and the only reason your heart beats 60 times a minute is because God has his hand wrapped around it. The fact is, everything you have materially is yours because God gave it to you.

God gives us everything for our joy

In some circles, God has a reputation as a killjoy: if he gives us good things, it's only because he feels he must, and he certainly doesn't want us to enjoy life. But nothing could be further from the truth. Look at Paul's description of God's generosity in 1 Timothy:

> Command those who are rich in this present world not to be arrogant nor to put their hope in wealth, which is so uncertain, but to put their hope in God, who richly provides us with everything for our enjoyment. (1 Tim 6:17)

God richly provides us with everything we have *for our joy*. God loves giving.

I'm part of a family with Irish roots. When my parents moved to Australia in the 1960s, my mum had already learned some Irish at school back in Ireland, and some words stuck with her and entered the family vernacular. For example, a 'gurrier' is a lout, a worthless person. I often heard this word when I had my hand in the biscuit tin: "Get out of it, you gurrier!" Another favourite was 'sui sios' (pronounced *see she-us*). It means "sit down" (I also heard that a lot, especially at dinner time). But my favourite word was 'flahoolick'. 'Flahoolick' means 'over-the-top, almost irresponsibly generous'. The man who shouts the whole bar a drink—he's 'flahoolick'. The granny who turns up on Christmas Day laden with gifts for the grandkids, far more than they need or she can afford—she's 'flahoolick'.

The Bible teaches that God is flahoolick. He's over-the-top generous. We live in an almost embarrassingly abundant world, because God loves us.

That's not to say there aren't problems in our world: millions of people still go hungry, and that's awful. But economists agree this is not because there isn't enough to go around in the world; it's because many of us take too much for ourselves. God made a generous, abundant world because he's a generous, abundant God. The fact that some of us don't have as much as others—or enough at all—isn't because God hasn't given us enough. It's often because we haven't shared it well enough. The problem is not with God's generosity; he has given us *everything* we have materially, and he's given it to us *for our joy*.

Every spiritual blessing

But God hasn't just given us everything we have materially. He's also given us everything we have spiritually.

Look at how Paul expresses this in Ephesians 1: "Praise be to the God and Father of our Lord Jesus Christ, who has blessed us in the heavenly realms with every spiritual blessing in Christ" (v 3). God has given us *every* spiritual blessing in Christ. Not *some* spiritual blessings; not the spiritual blessings he found at the bottom of the drawer and didn't want anymore. No, *every* spiritual blessing we need to live a full life with God, both now and forever, he has given to us in Christ.

Let's list just some of these blessings:

> He chose us in [Christ] before the creation of the world to be holy and blameless in his sight. (v 4)

> He predestined us for adoption to sonship through Jesus Christ ... (v 5)

> In [Christ] we have redemption through his blood, the forgiveness of sins, in accordance with the riches of God's grace that he lavished on us. (vv 7–8)
>
> He made known to us the mystery of his will according to his good pleasure, which he purposed in Christ, to be put into effect when the times reach their fulfilment—to bring unity to all things in heaven and on earth under Christ. (vv 9–10)

Holiness, blamelessness, adoption, redemption, forgiveness, revelation: God has given us all these things and more! God has given us *everything* we need spiritually.

What's more, he's given us these gifts for free. All this blessing is the result of "the riches of God's grace that he lavished on us" (vv 7–8). And yet, though it cost us nothing, it cost God everything. God redeemed us "through [Jesus'] blood" (v 7). God gave us every spiritual blessing, but it cost him the life of his Son.

We were made to love and serve God. But instead, we worshipped created things, not the Creator. Talking about humanity, Paul says, "They exchanged the truth about God for a lie, and worshipped and served created things rather than the Creator —who is forever praised" (Rom 1:25). That is, we loved things rather than the one who gave them to us.

To extend the Christmas analogy, it's like we fell so in love with Granny's gifts that we ignored Granny, and when she tried to talk to us, we told her to shut up and leave us alone so we could play with the soccer ball she'd given us. That's not why she gave us the ball; she gave it to us to bring us closer together. But we used her gift in a way that drove us apart.

So it is with God. As a human race, we love the things God has made more than we love him, and we've ignored him. But in his overwhelming, lavish, flahoolick love, God has given us his Son, because he wants to forgive us and restore us to relationship with him and give us every spiritual blessing.

Paul puts it so well in 2 Corinthians:

> For you know the grace of our Lord Jesus Christ, that though he was rich, yet for your sake he became poor, so that you through his poverty might become rich. (2 Cor 8:9)

We had nothing. Jesus had everything. But he gave up everything for us so we might have the 'everything' of full relationship with God. And he did it for our joy. God is a giver.

Therefore, we should give because ...

God has given us everything we have, materially and spiritually, for our joy.

So how should this motivate *us* to give?

We understand how it would motivate us to give if we had to *earn* God's approval, because giving might earn us 'points' with God. But how does the fact we *already* have God's approval, in Jesus, motivate us to give? If God wanted us to be generous, hasn't he shot himself in the foot by making salvation free? Why should we give? How does *grace* make us give?

The Bible gives us two answers.

We're grateful

The first answer is very simple: we're so grateful for what God has given us that we are moved to give too.

There's a wonderful example of this in Luke 7, where a woman who is a notorious sinner crashes a party that some Pharisees have given for Jesus. She brings a bottle of expensive perfume and lavishly pours it over Jesus' feet. It's a very generous act—but why does she do it? Because she's grateful. This sinful woman knows Jesus has come to offer forgiveness to people just like her, and so she responds by giving him a gift. Jesus puts it this way: "Therefore, I tell you, her many sins have been forgiven—as her great love has shown. But whoever has been forgiven little loves little" (v 47). She's grateful, and this moves her to generosity.

There's something deeply transformative about

gratitude. *Les Misérables* is the story of Jean Valjean, a thief who's been in prison for 19 years for his crimes. When he is finally released, he is taken in by a kindly bishop, who gives him food, lodging and love. But old habits die hard, and in the middle of the night Valjean steals the bishop's silverware and runs off. He's soon captured and returned to the bishop so the police can confirm the goods are stolen. But then something astonishing happens: instead of condemning him by confirming the silverware is stolen, the bishop tells the police he gave it to Valjean. As the officers look on, he then gives Valjean two valuable candlesticks, saying that he forgot to take them. The police accept the story and leave. Once they're alone, the bishop then speaks to Valjean: God has spared his (Valjean's) life, so he must sell the candlesticks, use the proceeds to establish himself, and live a good life from now on. And that's what Valjean does. He becomes a good man—and eventually a rich man who uses his riches for good. An act of grace—of being given to—launches Valjean into a life of giving, because he is grateful.

It's the same with us: God has given to us in such a flahoolick and undeserved way, so we should be grateful, and that gratefulness should flow over into a new life of generosity.

But there's a second answer to the question of why we should give—one that is very closely related to the first answer.

Grace changes us

When God gave to us in the gospel, he did something more than just forgive our sins: he freed us to be the people we were always made to be—people made in his image. And that means freeing us to be givers, because God is a giver. We give in response to God's giving, not just because we're grateful, but because the gospel has changed us to be more like God, who is the ultimate giver.

We see this very clearly in Ephesians 4–5. Without the work of God in the gospel, humanity is greedy: "Having lost all sensitivity, they have given themselves over to sensuality so as to indulge in every kind of impurity, and they are full of greed" (Eph 4:19). This is the human condition outside of Christ.

But once we've been forgiven, we no longer need to live that way. Rather, "you were taught, with regard to your former way of life, to put off your old self, which is being corrupted by its deceitful desires ... and to put on the new self, created to be like God in true righteousness and holiness" (Eph 4:22, 24). In other words, when God forgives us, he also enables us to start being who we were always meant be—people made in his image: "to be like God in true righteousness and holiness".

And because God is a giver, part of us becoming more like him means being givers: "Anyone who has been stealing must steal no longer, but must work, doing something useful with their own hands, that they may have something to share with those in need" (Eph 4:28). We don't just give because we're grateful to God for what he's given us. We give because what he's given us—the gospel—also transforms us to be more like him. Thus, we give because God gives. As Paul concludes: "Follow God's example, therefore, as dearly loved children and walk in the way of love, just as Christ loved us and gave himself up for us as a fragrant offering and sacrifice to God" (Eph 5:1–2).

This same attitude runs throughout the New Testament. We are to put the interests of others ahead of our own, just as Jesus did not look to his own interests in giving his life for us (Phil 2:1–8). We are to use our freedom to love and serve one another, not to serve ourselves (Gal 5:13–15). We are to be like our heavenly Father, who generously "causes his sun to rise on the evil and the good, and sends rain on the righteous and the unrighteous" (Matt 5:45). But we can only do these things when we have been transformed at a deep level—moved away from the greedy, inward-looking tendencies of the sinful human heart, and moved to become like the God who saved us by his grace and gave us every good gift for our joy.

Why should we give? Because God has given to us, both materially and spiritually, for our joy. And this changes us. Not only are we so moved by gratitude that we want to become generous in response, but we are transformed at a deep level, where our hearts are changed as God slowly makes us more like himself. And so we give, because God is a giver.

We are not made for a small life, a life of selfish pleasures. We are made for a big life, a noble life, a generous life, because we're made in the image of a big, noble, generous God. What better reason is there to give than that?

So as we finish this chapter, let this be our prayer: "LORD, the God of our fathers Abraham, Isaac and Israel, keep these desires and thoughts in the hearts of your people forever, and keep [our] hearts loyal to you" (1 Chron 29:18)

2 | How much should we give?

We saw in the last chapter *why* Christians should give: because God has given to us, materially and spiritually, and this both *makes us grateful* and *transforms us* to be people who are more like our generous God.

But this leads to the obvious question: If we're to give, *how much* should we give?

The first thing to say is that we do a disservice to the Bible's teaching on generosity if we jump straight to the category of money. The gospel transforms us so that we are free to be generous in every way, just as God is generous to us in every way. That might look like giving time, or showing hospitality, or using our gifts generously in church, or all manner of other things we could do. The generosity of God should drive us to be lavish, and to be creative in looking for ways to be generous. Don't fall into the trap of limiting your pursuit of generosity to money.

But that still leaves us with the very important question of money, which is the focus of this book. Specifically, how much money should we give?

I'm conscious that this is a question that might make some of us nervous. We're often told not to talk about money, and that how much we give should be entirely a matter of personal conscience. We're therefore nervous when anyone—even in a book—starts 'telling' us how much we should give (or what to do with our money at all).

But if we're going to think about money and generosity, there's no point in shying away from the practical reality: we will need to decide how much to give. More importantly, Jesus has plenty to say about money. In fact, it's estimated that half of Jesus' parables either are about money or at least touch on the topic of money. Clearly, he thinks it's something we need to think about.

Why is this? Because money is a deeply spiritual issue. In fact, according to Jesus, our attitude to money is one of the best barometers of our spiritual condition. Let me explain.

According to Jesus, there is a war going on inside us for our worship—a war between God and money. Jesus says:

> "No-one can serve two masters. Either you will hate the one and love the other, or you will be devoted to the one and despise

> the other. You cannot serve both God and money." (Matt 6:24)

Of all the potential alternative masters to God in the world, the one Jesus says is most likely to claim our allegiance is not work or family or sex, but money. Why?

It's because of what money represents. Money simply stands in for all the other *things* in the world. Money was invented so that when you wanted to buy something, you didn't need to drag your cow or house along with you to exchange it. You could simply bring your money and give it to the seller, and they could then use that money to buy their own cow or house. It's much easier to put coins in your pocket than cattle or houses! And so money was invented to stand in for *things*.

Now this would be fine if not for the fact that sinful human beings have a major problem with *things*. Basically, we've fallen in love with them in an unhealthy way. As we saw in our last chapter, God says humans have "exchanged the truth about God for a lie, and worshipped and served created things rather than the Creator" (Rom 1:25). We live for the things God gives us rather than for God himself. And because of this, we also worship money, because money stands for *things*. It gives us ready access to whichever *things* we think will make us happy or secure or attractive or powerful or fulfilled. It's why God's word is so stark in saying that greed "*is* idolatry" (Col 3:5) and that a greedy person "*is* an idolater" (Eph 5:5).

You can see why greed is a worship issue. There's a battle going on inside us over who we will build our lives around, who we will make our master. And because of sin—our distorted love of the good things God has given us—money is God's chief opponent in this war.

It's crucial to know all this before we ask, "How much should I give?" because it's not a question being asked in neutral territory. It's a question being asked in the middle of a war where our natural, sinful tendency will always be to worship money, and hence we'll be reluctant to give it away. The perceived self-sufficiency it offers, or a sense of independence or security or status—these are examples of the *things* money promises, which will make it hard for us to part with it.

This is why the Bible's eventual answer to the question "How much should I give?" is so amazing: *Give whatever your heart chooses to give.*

Given everything we've just seen about the war we're in, how can this be?

Give whatever your heart chooses to give

The New Testament never gives a percentage of our income that we're meant to give away to other people. For example, Paul asks the Corinthian church to contribute to a collection he is taking up for the church in Jerusalem, which has been hit by a famine.[2] In 1 Corinthians, Paul tells them to set aside an amount each week for the collection, in keeping with their income (1 Cor 16:1–3), and in 2 Corinthians he reminds them to keep giving to the collection and says that a group led by Titus will be there to pick it up soon (8:10–9:5). But here's the key point: he never once tells them how much to give. He never gives a number or a percentage. In fact, he explicitly says that, though he wants them to "excel in this grace of giving" (8:7), he is "not commanding" them about it (8:8).

This lightness of touch when it comes to giving runs all through 2 Corinthians 8–9.

The Macedonians only gave what they wanted to give to the Jerusalem collection. They gave out of "overflowing joy" (8:2). "*Entirely on their own,* they *urgently pleaded* with [Paul] for the *privilege* of sharing in this service to the Lord's people" (8:3–4). They gave, first and foremost, not out of a desire to serve Paul but out of a desire to serve God (8:5). In other words, the Macedonians were not forced to give; they gave freely, from the desire of their hearts.

Likewise, Paul tells the Corinthians that their

2 See Acts 11:28, 24:17; Rom 15:26.

giving is to flow from the desire of their hearts. The year before, the Corinthians had been "the first not only to give but also to have the desire to do so" (8:10)—a fact Paul clearly commends. They had (and have) an "eager willingness" to give (8:11; see also 9:2). Paul wants to encourage this. He wants their donation to "be ready as a generous gift, not as one grudgingly given" (9:5). "Each of you should give what you have decided in your heart to give, not reluctantly or under compulsion, for God loves a cheerful giver" (9:7).

Paul couldn't be clearer: the Corinthians are free to decide how much they should give.

This is very different from the Old Testament, where the basic principle was the 'tithe', which means 10 percent. So for the Old Testament Israelite:

> "A tithe of everything from the land, whether grain from the soil or fruit from the trees, belongs to the LORD; it is holy to the LORD. Whoever would redeem any of their tithe must add a fifth of the value to it. Every tithe of the herd and flock—every tenth animal that passes under the shepherd's rod—will be holy to the LORD. No-one may pick out the good from the bad or make any substitution. If anyone does make a substitution, both the animal and its substitute become holy and cannot be redeemed." (Lev 27:30–33)

So that's the required 'giving amount' for an Israelite: 10 percent. And there's no flexibility. They even put in a rule to stop people gaming the system: the choice of which animal to give is completely randomized, so people can't choose only to give away the bad ones. And if they do try, there's a penalty: they must give away both the bad animal and another one.

But that's not the only amount an Israelite had to give. There was giving to support the Levites in their work in the temple, giving to God at festivals, and giving for the poor and outcasts. In other words, they had to give away quite a bit.

The key is that the figure was always set. The percentage was never left up to individuals.

Why?

It's not because the New Testament is better than the Old Testament. The same God wrote both Testaments and rules the people of both. It's because in the Old Testament the Holy Spirit had not yet been poured out on all God's people, and their hearts were hard. God draws a clear distinction between Old and New Testament believers: they are both saved, but New Testament believers have *all* been given God's Spirit. As Paul says, "When you believed, you were marked in [Jesus] with a seal, the promised Holy Spirit" (Eph 1:13b). That is, *all* Christians have the Holy Spirit. So now, as we walk by the Spirit, he enables us not to "gratify the desires of the flesh" (Gal 5:16), but instead to display the fruit of the Spirit: "love, joy, peace, forbearance, kindness, goodness, faithfulness, gentleness and self-control" (Gal 5:22–23). We can serve God in the way he wants us to serve him because he's given us his Spirit.

It's not that the Spirit wasn't at work in people *at all* in the Old Testament. He was. He came upon kings (e.g. 1 Sam 11:6, 16:13), prophets (e.g. Ezek 2:2), and others (e.g. Num 27:18; Judg 3:10) to help them do specific jobs. But he didn't come upon *everyone*, and even those he did come upon he sometimes left (e.g. 1 Sam 16:14). Old Testament believers didn't have the Spirit's help in the same way we do when it comes to doing what God wants—including being generous. They had to be *told* how much to give, because they couldn't be trusted to be generous on their own.

But now that God has poured out his Spirit on *all* believers, he can work in our hearts to make us more like him, including making us more generous. And because of that, he now doesn't have to say, "Give X percent". He just says, "I've forgiven you and poured out my Spirit upon you. So give what you want."

What's the rule for Christians? *Give whatever your heart chooses to give.*

Ask God to enlarge your heart

But here's a challenge God also gives to his people: be willing to enlarge your heart.[3] Or, perhaps more accurately, ask God to do a miracle and enlarge your heart. Ask God to change you so that you want to be more generous.

There is, of course, a risk in God not giving us percentages for giving: we could take it as an opportunity to be stingy. But if we truly know the grace of God, and if we know who he is changing us to be, we won't want to use our freedom to give as little as possible; we'll want to use it to give as *much* as possible. We'll know we only need to give what we want, but we'll always want to give more. We'll *want* to want to give more. We'll want our hearts to grow.

In 2 Corinthians 8–9, it's true that Paul only wants the Corinthians to give freely. But he also wants them to "excel" in the "grace of giving": "But since you excel in everything—in faith, in speech, in knowledge, in complete earnestness and in the love we have kindled in you—see that you also excel in this grace of giving" (8:7). Likewise, even as Paul has commended the Corinthians for their willingness to give to the Jerusalem collection, he

3 I'm indebted to Andrew Heard for a series of sermons on this topic, in which I first heard the formulation 'Give whatever your heart chooses, but be willing to enlarge your heart'.

also doesn't want them to get cold feet when the time comes for their gift to be collected:

> And here is my judgement about what is best for you in this matter. Last year you were the first not only to give but also to have the desire to do so. Now finish the work, so that your eager willingness to do it may be matched by your completion of it, according to your means. (8:10–11)

So while Paul wants the Corinthians to give willingly—what their hearts choose—he also wants them to excel in giving, and to *actually* give. He wants their hearts to grow.

The power of godly example

How does God enlarge our hearts? The Bible doesn't lead us to believe that God will simply zap our hearts so that we instantly become generous. Rather, he typically does this work in two ways.

The first way God changes our hearts is by showing us *the power of godly example.*

This may happen through comparing us to other generous people, which motivates our hearts to become more like theirs.

This is part of Paul's approach in 2 Corinthians 8, where he seeks to motivate the church in Corinth to generosity by comparing them with other generous people: "I am not commanding you, but I want to test the sincerity of your love by comparing it with the earnestness of others" (v 8). He gives two examples in the chapter. The first is the Macedonian churches (the Philippians and Thessalonians):

> And now, brothers and sisters, we want you to know about the grace that God has given the Macedonian churches. In the midst of a very severe trial, their overflowing joy and their extreme poverty welled up in rich generosity. For I testify that they gave as much as they were able, and even beyond their ability. Entirely on their own, they urgently pleaded with us for the privilege of sharing in this service to the Lord's people. And they exceeded our expectations: They gave themselves first of all to the Lord, and then by the will of God also to us. (vv 1–5)

As we've already seen, the Macedonians were willing and eager to give. But they were also extremely poor and under great trial (v 2). Yet despite that, they gave as much as they could, and even more than they were able (v 3). In other words, they had small wallets, but big hearts. They were genuinely flahoolick. And Paul uses their example to grow the Corinthians' hearts, to compare their love "with the earnestness of others".

The second example Paul gives is Jesus himself.

Jesus is very different from the Macedonians: he was rich. Yet he also had a big heart, wanted to serve others, and was willing to suffer for it:

> For you know the grace of our Lord Jesus Christ, that though he was rich, yet for your sake he became poor, so that you through his poverty might become rich. (v 9)

Let's dig into this wonderful verse in a little more detail.

"Though he was rich ..."

To say that Jesus was rich must be the biggest understatement of all time. Think about the riches Jesus had before becoming human: He was, in Paul's words elsewhere, "in very nature God" (Phil 2:6). That means Jesus made and owned the universe. It's estimated that there are around 200 billion trillion stars in the cosmos. Jesus owned them all. Time, matter, antimatter, dark matter, energy, dark energy, gravity, electromagnetism, the strong and weak nuclear forces: they were all his. Before his incarnation, Jesus was rich. There's no-one richer than the maker of the universe.

"Yet he became poor ..."

But read on in Philippians 2:6–7: "[Jesus], being in very nature God, did not consider equality with God something to be used to his own advantage;

rather, he made himself nothing by taking the very nature of a servant, being made in human likeness". God the Son became human. The Lord of space and time became a person—a person who had to sleep, and became hungry and thirsty, and needed time by himself, just like us. Can you imagine?

And he died—not just any death, but the most shameful death possible: "And being found in appearance as a man, he humbled himself by becoming obedient to death—even death on a cross!" (Phil 2:8)

There is no *richer* person than the owner of the universe. And there is no *poorer* person than a man on a cross. Yet that's what Jesus became for us. For our sake he became poor, so that through his poverty we might become rich. Through his death on the cross, Jesus paid for our sin so we could be forgiven and have the riches of God's mercy. That's Jesus' heart.

So how much should you give? Simple: give whatever your heart chooses to give. But don't ever use that as an excuse to be miserly. Instead, be eager and willing for God to enlarge your heart.

How does that happen? First and foremost, it's God's generosity to us in Christ that will transform our hearts to make us generous. As we've seen from 2 Corinthians 8, Christ became poor for us so that we could become rich. God enlarges our hearts by taking this truth and embedding it deeply into our minds and hearts so that we might be transformed by it.

Second, let the bigness of other people's hearts enlarge your own heart. Just as Paul was greatly encouraged by the Macedonians and their generosity—expecting the Corinthians to be similarly affected—so we can be encouraged by the generosity of God's people. This won't always be easy to see, largely because Jesus tells his people to give in secret, seeking the approval of their heavenly Father rather than other people. But whenever we see God's people being generous, we should allow our hearts to be warmed and enlarged by the ways in which God has changed them.

Providing for us as we are generous

The second big way God enlarges our hearts is by promising to look after us if we are generous:

> Remember this: Whoever sows sparingly will also reap sparingly, and whoever sows generously will also reap generously. Each of you should give what you have decided in your heart to give, not reluctantly or under compulsion, for God loves a cheerful giver. And God is able to bless you abundantly, so that in all things at all times, having all that you need, you will abound in every good work. (2 Cor 9:6–8)

The thing that enables us to be generous givers is the 'safety net' of knowing that God will look after us even if we are generous. We can give because God will give us "all that [we] need", even after we've given. Being generous doesn't mean we'll miss out:

> Now he who supplies seed to the sower and bread for food will also supply and increase your store of seed and will enlarge the harvest of your righteousness. You will be enriched in every way so that you can be generous on every occasion, and through us your generosity will result in thanksgiving to God. (2 Cor 9:10–11)

Our generosity will be good for our hearts (God will "enlarge the harvest of your righteousness"), but our bellies won't miss out either (he will "increase your store of seed"). We can afford to be generous because God will still look after us once we've been generous.

A couple of caveats are important here.

First, this is not a version of the 'prosperity gospel'. Paul is not teaching that God will make every Christian rich, or that Christians should give to become rich. On the contrary, God give us all that we *need* (v 8), not everything we might want. What's more, this passage explicitly teaches that God will give us what we need not so that we might gain more for ourselves, but so that we might have enough to keep giving: "Having all that you need, you will abound in every good work" (v 8). "You will be enriched in every way so that you can be generous on every occasion" (v 11). God looks after us so we can keep giving, not so that we can gain more for ourselves.

Second, it's true that some Christians, despite these promises, still have very little materially. In such cases, God doesn't seem to have given these brothers and sisters "all that [they] need". What are we to do with this?

There is not the space here to get into a full-blown discussion of Christian poverty and God's material care for Christians. Suffice to say, some Christians will be very poor—the Macedonians being a case in point. In these cases, God only tells Christians to give according to their means (2 Cor 8:11). "For if the willingness is there, the gift is acceptable according to what one has, not according to what one does not have" (8:12).

Even so, Christians may still decide to give beyond their means—again, like the Macedonians, who "gave as much as they were able, and even beyond their ability" (8:3). In this case, their giving may have brought a measure of suffering. But material compensation is not the only thing God promises to generous Christian givers. He also promises to enlarge the harvest of their *righteousness* (9:10). Therefore, we can assume that even though the Macedonians chose to give beyond their means, they still thought it was worthwhile because of the honour of being able to give and the thanksgiving to God that it brought (9:11). All things considered, they still believed that they came out 'ahead' when they gave.

So how much should we give? Whatever our heart chooses to give. But we must be willing for God to enlarge our hearts, so that we always want to give more (even if we can't). How does God enlarge our hearts? By getting us to compare our hearts with the hearts of others who are generous, and by promising to look after us—materially, but even more importantly, spiritually—when we give, so that we will be confident and joyful to give.

3 | Who should we give to?

We saw in our first chapter *why* Christians should give: because God has given to us. And we saw in our second chapter *how much* Christians should give: as much as our heart chooses to give, but always wanting God to enlarge our hearts.

But that leaves one last question: *Who should we give to?*

That's not an idle question, because there are so many good things that could be the focus of our generosity. Churches, mission organizations, aid agencies, the local animal shelter, groups that fight human trafficking—they and countless others all ask for our support. And we want to give to them all! But we have a limited amount of money, so we need to make choices. How do we make these choices without feeling paralyzed about our decisions before we've made them, or guilty about our decisions after they're made?

Is the Bible any help in this situation? Does it

teach us who to give to and how to prioritize them?

Thankfully, the answers are yes and yes!

The first thing to say is that, very broadly speaking, the Bible pushes us to focus our generous giving on people. How can we be generous in a way that blesses and cares for other people? But that's such a broad category as to be almost useless in directing our giving. So which people, or what kinds of people, should be the focus of our generosity?

Biological family

The first group of people the Bible says we should give to is our biological family.

Writing to Timothy in Ephesus, Paul gives these instructions:

> Give proper recognition to those widows who are really in need. But if a widow has children or grandchildren, these should learn first of all to put their religion into practice by caring for their own family and so repaying their parents and grandparents, for this is pleasing to God ... Anyone who does not provide for their relatives, and especially for their own household, has denied the faith and is worse than an unbeliever. (1 Tim 5:3–4, 8)

The context here is that there are poor widows in the church, and the church is trying to work out who should care for them. The answer is: if the widows have no family, the church should care for them; if they do have family, their family should care for them. The clear implication is that believers should care for and provide for their own families. In fact, if we don't, we're "worse than an unbeliever".

This is not an excuse to spend *all* our money on our families at the expense of the rest of the world. We can't give our families the best of everything—overseas holidays, private school educations and the like—and give *nothing* to anyone else on the grounds that we're simply doing what the Bible says. That's just selfishness. Paul's instruction is about caring for widows who are in need and giving them enough money to *live*, not to *live for pleasure* (see 1 Tim 5:6). We should ensure that our family has everything they *need*, not everything they *want*.

The needy

The second group of people the Bible says we should give to is those we might simply classify as 'the needy'. This group, covering a range of people with material needs, can be broken down into two sub-groups: needy Christians and needy non-Christians.

Needy Christians

> This is how we know what love is: Jesus Christ laid down his life for us. And we ought to lay

> down our lives for our brothers and sisters. If anyone has material possessions and sees a brother or sister in need but has no pity on them, how can the love of God be in that person? Dear children, let us not love with words or speech but with actions and in truth. (1 John 3:16–18)

John clearly calls for us to give to needy "brothers and sisters"—a way of referring to fellow disciples of Jesus. We shouldn't notice Christians in need and just feel warmly towards them; we should provide for their needs. This is because Jesus didn't show his love for us just by feeling warmly towards us. He laid down his life for us. So we're to do the same for other Christians. If we see a Christian in need, we're to do what we can to meet those practical needs (as we saw from the Macedonian Christians in the previous chapter). Only then can we say we are truly loving them.

This has lots of applications in real life.

For example, there are sure to be financially needy people in your local church from time to time. How can you help them? It could be that your church sets up an emergency relief fund for members who are facing hardship and need help paying the next major bill. Or it could be that you, personally, find out about someone's need and decide to give to them, either in cash or in kind. There are myriad ways we can care for the poorer members of our church. How could you do it?

There will also be many other Christians with financial and material needs—in your local community, around your country, and overseas. One way to help meet these needs is to partner with organizations that have been established to provide aid. For example, Open Doors is a ministry that cares for overseas Christians who are poor because they're Christians—that is, because they're persecuted for their faith in Jesus. Before writing this book, I gave little thought to my obligation to care for the specifically Christian poor. But as I searched the Scriptures on the topic of generosity and giving, my attitude changed. As a result, we've now changed our family budget to include gifts to needy believers overseas. Could you do the same?

Needy non-Christians

We're also to give to needy people generally, no matter what their beliefs:

> Let us not become weary in doing good, for at the proper time we will reap a harvest if we do not give up. Therefore, as we have opportunity, let us do good to all people, especially to those who belong to the family of believers. (Gal 6:9–10)

Yes, we should care *especially* for believers. But we should also care for *all people*.

Wherever Christians have lived this way, they

have had a significant impact on their culture and their society. And from the earliest days, Christians (at our best) have cared for the needy around us. For example, in the time of the Roman Empire, Christians and churches set up orphanages, food banks, hospitals and much more. In fact, they did it so much that, in AD 362, the Roman Emperor Julian the Apostate complained to his pagan priests that Christians were making them look bad. He wrote: "It is disgraceful that, when no Jew ever has to beg, and the impious Galileans [i.e. Christians] support not only their own poor but ours as well, all men see our people lack aid from us".[4] Clearly, the church's charity to all people—not just fellow believers—had an impact on the wider world.

In our family, we've tried to live this out in how we shape our giving portfolio. We give to some charities that are focused on caring for Christians, but we also give to charities that provide aid for anyone, regardless of belief. Generally, we like to give to Christian charities that combine both practical aid and gospel witness to these people. We do this because, if at all possible, we want the aid's recipients to know *why* they're being helped and to know the deeper hope of the gospel. But we also know there are some countries that won't allow Christian aid agencies to operate freely (such as

4 DF Caner, 'The undeserving poor', *Christian History Institute*, 2020 (christianhistoryinstitute.org/magazine/article/the-undeserving-poor).

some very strict Muslim countries), yet whose people are still in great need. Should we choose not give to them because our giving will never be linked with the gospel? No. They are needy people, made and loved by God, and we still want to care for them, even if we can only do so materially. And so, because of this conviction, we give a small part of our annual giving to charities that work in places that Christian charities can't reach.

The work of the gospel

The third cause the Bible says we should give to is gospel work. This can be broken down into two sub-categories: the gospel work of the local church and the gospel work of other groups, such as mission agencies.

Before going on, it's worth defining what I mean by 'gospel work'. I'm talking about the work of gospel *proclamation*: any work where the core business is teaching the Bible and *telling* people, both Christians and non-Christians, about Jesus.

It's important to distinguish the work of gospel proclamation from other work. Being a dentist or a plumber, for example, is good work, and can be done for the glory of God. In fact, this applies to everything in life: "Whether you eat or drink or whatever you do, do it *all* for the glory of God" (1 Cor 10:31). Paul writes something similar in Colossians: "Whatever you do, whether in word or deed, do it *all* in the name of the Lord Jesus, giving thanks to God the Father through him" (Col 3:17). Whatever my job—dentist, plumber, homemaker, pastor—I want to do it "in the name of the Lord" and for his glory.

But there's another type of work—a type that the Bible calls "the work of the Lord". In 1 Corinthians, Paul writes to the church in Corinth: "When Timothy comes, see to it that he has nothing to fear while he is with you, for he is carrying on *the work of the Lord*, just as I am" (1 Cor 16:10). What is this work? In context, it's clear that it's gospel preaching. Paul uses the same term in the previous chapter while explaining the significance of the resurrection:

> Therefore, my dear brothers and sisters, stand firm. Let nothing move you. Always give yourselves fully to *the work of the Lord*, because you know that your labour in the Lord is not in vain. (1 Cor 15:58)[5]

The Corinthians are to give themselves wholeheartedly to "the work of the Lord"—gospel proclamation—because it's the only work where the fruit will last forever. Why? Because its fruit is *people*. It's only people who will be resurrected and live on

5 For more on "the work of the Lord" as specific gospel work, see P Orr, 'Abounding in the work of the Lord (1 Cor 15:58): Everything we do as Christians or specific gospel work?', *Themelios*, 2013, 38(2):205–214 (thegospelcoalition.org/themelios/article/abounding-in-the-work-of-the-lord-1-cor-1558-everything-we-do-as-christians).

into eternity—not the houses we build, the novels we write, or any other work we do.

This doesn't mean we should give up what I will (for the sake of convenience) call 'regular' work, such as dentistry, plumbing, or poetry writing. It is good and important work, and it can glorify God. Back in Colossians 3, Paul writes these stirring words:

> Whatever you do, work at it with all your heart, as *working for the Lord*, not for human masters, since you know that you will receive an inheritance from the Lord as a reward. It is the Lord Christ you are serving. (vv 23–24)

Any work we do is done *for* the Lord. This work is also necessary: we need poets, dentists and plumbers in order for life to function. But it is *different* from gospel work. Dentistry is good, but it doesn't help anyone be reconciled to God. Plumbing is necessary, but our plumbing won't last into eternity; only people will do that—those who respond rightly to the good news of Jesus being raised to everlasting life, and those who don't being separated from the goodness of God forever (see Dan 12:2). So we all need to do regular work (work *for* the Lord), but we also *all* need to do gospel work (the work *of* the Lord).

And the New Testament is clear that a key part of doing the work of the Lord is partnering financially in the work of the Lord. So what sorts of gospel work should we give to?

Gospel work in the local church

> The elders who direct the affairs of the church well are worthy of double honour, especially those whose work is preaching and teaching. For Scripture says, "Do not muzzle an ox while it is treading out the grain," and "The worker deserves his wages." (1 Tim 5:17–18)

Paul tells Timothy that the elders of the church, especially those who preach and teach the Bible, are worthy of "double honour" (v 17). The next verse explains what this "double honour" means by quoting two Scriptures: "Do not muzzle an ox while it is treading out the grain" (Deut 25:4) and "the worker deserves his wages" (Luke 10:7). The quote from Deuteronomy is about caring for animals while they work for you: instead of muzzling them, let them eat the grain that falls in front of them while they mill. In the quote from Luke, Jesus sends his disciples out on mission, telling them that those who benefit from their ministry should provide for their material needs. Putting these two quotes together, along with Paul's own comments, the point is clear: the people of God should provide for the financial and material needs of those who lead the church, especially those who preach and teach the word of God.

In another key passage, 1 Corinthians 9, Paul says that although he doesn't want to receive payment for preaching the gospel in this situation, as a preacher he is entitled to do so. Why? Because gospel preaching gives people a spiritual benefit, so preachers are entitled to a material benefit:

> If we have sown spiritual seed among you, is it too much if we reap a material harvest from you? If others have this right of support from you, shouldn't we have it all the more? ... the Lord has commanded that those who preach the gospel should receive their living from the gospel. (vv 11–12, 14)

In summary, Paul says that church leaders are entitled to be paid for their work.

This is in large part because of what the church *is*.

Earlier in 1 Timothy, Paul explains why he's writing: "Although I hope to come to you soon, I am writing you these instructions so that, if I am delayed, you will know how people ought to conduct themselves in God's household, which is the church of the living God, the pillar and foundation of the truth" (1 Tim 3:14–15).

Paul describes the church as "God's household" —God's family. And, as we've already seen above, Paul is about to instruct Timothy on the importance of caring for family (1 Tim 5:3–4, 8). Our fellow church members may not be our biological family, but they are our brothers and sisters in Christ. And so, just as we are called to care financially for our biological family, we are also called to care for our church family.

Paul also describes the church as the "pillar and foundation of the truth". It's not just another social club or doer of good in society. It's the guardian of the great hope of humanity, the gospel. It's the front line of God's rescue mission to the world. So it's vital that the church is led well. One way we can make sure that happens is to meet the financial and material needs of our church leaders (or at least some of them) so they can devote their time to its work.[6]

In this sense, giving to church—like giving to your family—is not so much an act of generosity as it is a duty and a responsibility. Christians have a duty to make sure that the household expenses are covered; we have a responsibility to care for our family members, both biological and spiritual.

6 It's important to emphasize that being paid as a church leader doesn't elevate you into some special spiritual class where you are above others in the church. It is simply a matter of the church paying some people so they can be freed up from regular work to give more of their time to gospel ministry. It's entirely possible for people to continue in paid 'regular' work while giving real leadership in the local church—as Paul seems to have done in Corinth, for example.

Gospel work beyond the local church

But we should also give generously to other gospel ministries, which may include supporting the work of churches beyond our own.

Paul writes the letter to the Philippians, to a church he planted in Philippi, from prison. He begins by thanking God for their "partnership in the gospel" (Phil 1:5), then concludes the letter by explaining what this partnership has involved: giving him money so he could plant more churches.

> As you Philippians know, in the early days of your acquaintance with the gospel, when I set out from Macedonia, not one church shared with me in the matter of giving and receiving, except you only; for even when I was in Thessalonica, you sent me aid more than once when I was in need. (Phil 4:15–16)

The Philippians partnered with Paul by sending him money to help him plant a church in Thessalonica.

Christians are not just to give towards the gospel work going on in their own churches, but also in the rest of the world, especially in places that have not yet heard the gospel.

There are endless possibilities, but here are just a few examples to fire your imagination:

- You could give to overseas mission. There are so many people in the world who don't know Jesus; nor do they even know a Christian who could tell them about Jesus. The need for world evangelization is urgent. Giving to overseas mission is one way to help this cause.
- You could give towards church planting in your area or around your country.
- You could give to parachurch organizations that do evangelism in places local churches can't reach, such as the local university Christian union.

God's vision is for all the world to hear the good news of Jesus, so it is good and right for us to give to the work of the gospel all over the world.

How do we prioritize?

So we should give to our family, to the needy (both Christians and non-Christians), and to gospel work (especially in our local church, but also further afield).

But that still leaves a problem: How do we choose between many good options? Most of us will only be able to give to a very small number of all the worthy causes before us. And even for the very wealthy Christian who can afford to give to many different causes, does the Bible say he or she should give more to some causes than to others? How do we prioritize our giving?

Thankfully, the Bible gives us help in this area.

First, there are some things we give to not so much out of generosity, but more out of duty. That is, it's not really optional to give to these things: it's compulsory.

The first of these, as we've already seen, is our family. If we don't provide for our family's basic needs, then we are "worse than an unbeliever" (1 Tim 5:8). But again, this is only for their basic needs; it's not an excuse to spend all our money on our families! For most of us in the West, this will still leave us with plenty to give to other causes. Yet it is important that we don't lose sight of this first priority: care for our families.

We also have a duty to our local church—our immediate family of believers, and the place where we receive our immediate spiritual benefit. Again, giving to the local church is not really optional.

Of course, it is possible to be generous (or to be stingy) in the *amount* that we give. What's more, God delights when we don't just give to church out of a sense of obligation, but when we give cheerfully—when our hearts are filled with delight at the privilege of giving to the work of the gospel. It would be a sad situation if we felt the same way about giving to church as we do about paying our power bill! Giving to our local church is not less than a duty, but it is so much more than a duty.

Yet it is also right to recognize this sense of

duty to our local church. Paul puts it bluntly: "If we have sown spiritual seed among you, is it too much if we reap a material harvest from you? ... the Lord has commanded that those who preach the gospel should receive their living from the gospel" (1 Cor 9:11, 14).

I sometimes hear Christians say they give to mission agencies and charities but not to their local church, because the gospel needs overseas are greater and there are plenty of people to support the local church. I can see some of the reasoning, and there certainly are needs elsewhere. But the local church is still to be our priority for giving (beyond our biological family). It's where we receive our immediate spiritual benefit, and so we have a duty to provide for it materially. It's the pillar and foundation of the truth in our local community, doing vitally important work. More pragmatically, if the members of a local church won't give to support its ministry, who else will? It needs our support. Although there are many other good things to give to, our local church should rightly come first in our giving.

Pastor John Piper puts it well:

> It's a helpful rule of thumb to say that, considering that this is your family of believers, with its own set of needs, and that you benefit from the church and give your life to it,

> starting with a tithe here is a good idea. And from there you can give more here and more elsewhere.[7]

Leaving the tithe question aside, that's very good advice.

So there are two things we must give to: our families (for their basic needs) and our local church. But many of us will still have money left over once we've given to these things, and there are still many other great needs. How should we prioritize these?

One helpful principle to help us decide is what we might call the *principle of eternity*. The principle of eternity would tell us that we should prioritize things that have an eternal impact over things that have a temporary impact.

You see this principle at work in Jesus' ministry. In Luke 4, Jesus has been healing people and then retreats to a quiet place, most likely to pray (see also Mark 1:35). But then a group of people find him and ask him to stay, presumably because they want him to keep healing. How does Jesus reply?

> "I must proclaim the good news of the kingdom of God to the other towns also, because that is why I was sent." And he kept

7 J Piper, 'Should all of my tithe go to the local church?', *Desiring God*, 14 April 2008 (desiringgod.org/interviews/should-all-of-my-tithe-go-to-the-local-church).

on preaching in the synagogues of Judea. (Luke 4:43–44)

Jesus loved healing people, and he loved preaching the gospel. But when he had to choose, he chose preaching. He made this choice because that is *why* he was sent: preaching was his main task. And it was his main task, presumably, because that was what would have an eternal impact, whereas physical healing would only have a temporary impact.

That doesn't mean Jesus was unconcerned about people's physical needs; nor does it mean that we should be indifferent to physical suffering. Healing the sick may not have been Jesus' top priority, but he still went out of his way to do it on numerous occasions. In some ways, proclaiming the gospel and helping people practically should not be seen as two different things. They should be understood as the same thing, done over two different time frames and with two different approaches: the (relative) short term of this age, where we seek to alleviate suffering in all kinds of ways; and the big picture of eternity, where we seek to alleviate suffering through preaching the gospel that can save people from their sins. Both have the very practical aim of ending suffering, whether in this world or in the world to come.

John Piper puts it like this: "The Bible teaches us to relieve as much suffering as we can both in this world and especially in the next".[8] Note the key word *especially*: it's important to help people avoid suffering now, but it's *more* important that we help them avoid suffering in hell, because it will be so much worse and last for so much longer. That's the *principle of eternity*.

And so our third priority, after providing for our family's basic needs and giving to our local church, should be giving to gospel work beyond our local church—overseas mission, university ministry, and the like. There's also the practical consideration mentioned above in our discussion about giving to the local church: many non-Christians will care about giving to needy people, but they will never care about giving to gospel work. If we don't do it, who will?

This still leaves giving to needy people, whether needy Christians or needy non-Christians. How should we prioritize these, as we have opportunity?

On balance, the priority should be needy Christians, given their proximity to us as our spiritual family. Look again at Paul's words in Galatians: "As we have opportunity, let us do good to all people, *especially* to those who belong to the family of believers" (Gal 6:10). This would place needy Christians as our fourth priority in giving.

8 J Piper, 'Prepare for suffering now', *Desiring God*, 18 August 2016 (desiringgod.org/interviews/prepare-for-suffering-now).

That means our fifth and final priority is needy non-Christians. While this group is last on our list, it is still very important to consider their needs. Yes, we're to give *especially* to Christians; but we're not to give *exclusively* to Christians. We're also to give to all people as we have opportunity, simply because they are our fellow image-bearers, and because the Bible tells us to. Just as God cares for all people, so should we.

So, to summarize in order, a biblically informed set of giving priorities would look like this:

1. Our biological family
2. Our local church
3. Other gospel ministries
4. Needy Christians
5. Needy non-Christians

Having said that, this list of priorities should not be understood as a set of absolutes that must apply to every Christian's giving in the same way. As God enlarges our hearts so that we can be generous as he is generous, some of us will be filled with a special desire to care for needy Christians (e.g. a church in a low-income country). Others will have a heart for needy non-Christians (e.g. child sponsorship). Others may feel especially drawn to support overseas gospel work, or evangelism within a particular subculture (e.g. athletes or artists). So long as we have considered the biblical priorities, and so long as we are not neglecting our obligations, we can rejoice at the diverse passions that God gives us. We can celebrate the way he cares for his world through the generosity of his people in countless different ways.

4 | What next?

We've seen *why* we give: because God has given to us, both materially and spiritually. We've seen *how much* we should give: whatever our hearts choose to give, but always wanting God to enlarge our hearts. And we've seen *who we should give to*: first to our family, then to the work of the gospel (in the local church first, then elsewhere) and then to the needy (Christians first, but also to everyone).

So what's next? How can we turn these principles into practices?

First, spend some time meditating on everything God has given you, and who he's made you to be in Christ. Don't skip over this step: remember, God is more interested in you than in what you can give; he wants your heart more than he wants your money. Before you start thinking about how much you will give or who you will give to, let his truths enlarge your heart and grow your love for him.

Second, roll up your sleeves and get practical. Open your budget and work out how much you can give away to other people. In our family, we do this towards the end of each year, planning for the next year. My wife and I work out what our combined incomes will be, what our major expenses will be, and how much we can give away (first as a percentage, then translated into a dollar amount). As you do this, try to push yourself towards being more generous than is comfortable. Work out a figure that is within your means (2 Cor 8:11) and that you won't resent giving away (2 Cor 9:7), but which also pushes you towards sacrifice ahead of comfort. After all, there is a war going on inside you that will naturally make you want to keep your money rather than give it away: fire a shot back at the enemy and push towards generosity rather than caution.

Third, it's time to get specific. Once you've worked out your giving figure for next year, work out who you're going to divide it between. This is the fun bit! In our family, we work out who we're going to give to in the four areas other than our family:

1. Church
2. Other gospel work
3. Needy Christians
4. Needy people generally

We then spread the total amount of our giving across the four areas, giving less to each area as we go down the list to reflect the priorities described in chapter 3. Again, this doesn't mean every individual or family must follow the same formula. But for us, it's been a helpful way to enact our convictions about the biblical priorities.

Fourth, once you've worked all this out, you just need to do it! I find putting a reminder in my calendar to give to one thing each month helps make sure I don't forget to give and that I don't end up with a large lump sum that needs to be given at the end of the year. Of course, you can also set up automatic transfers via the internet, which eliminates the risk of forgetting altogether. It's totally up to you—just do whatever works.

Of course, it might be that you're on a very low income and can't really afford to give much, or even anything at all. If that's genuinely your situation, that's okay (although almost everyone can afford to give something). Again, God is not after your money, but your heart. A willingness to give is just as valuable to the Lord as the giving—more valuable, in fact. Remember the poor widow who put two very small copper coins—much less than anyone else had given—into the temple treasury, and was warmly commended by Jesus:

> "This poor widow has put in more than all the others. All these people gave their gifts

> out of their wealth; but she out of her poverty put in all she had to live on." (Luke 21:3–4)

If you can't give much, think about other ways you can give. You can be generous with your time, your skills, or your possessions. There are lots of ways to be generous. Be creative! And of course, if you are in need yourself, don't be shy about asking people for help. Members of the church are here to support each other, and it's a wonderful expression of Christian unity.

The good news in all of this is that, whether we can give a lot or a little, giving is good for us: "It is more blessed to give than to receive" (Acts 20:35). I hope you find that to be true as you keep giving to the world around you, and as you enjoy the gifts God has given to you.

In other words, I hope you enjoy being a cheerful giver.

How to Walk into Church

By Tony Payne

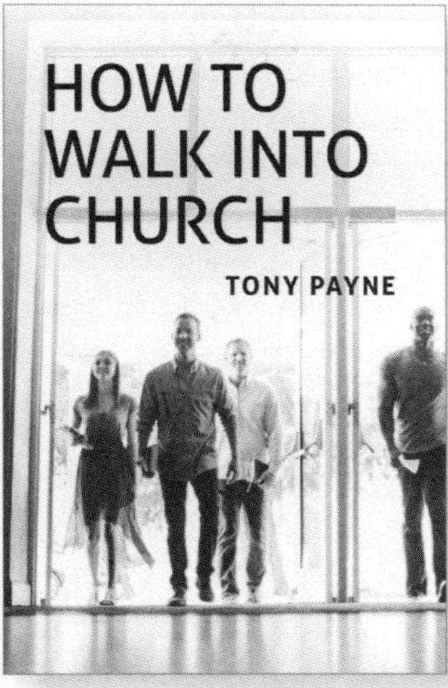

If you've been a churchgoer for more than just a few Sundays, walking into church probably doesn't seem like it deserves its own 'how to' manual. It most likely seems like a pretty straightforward and trivial weekly activity. But how you walk into church reveals a great deal about what you think church is, what it's for, and what you think you're doing there.

In *How to Walk into Church*, Tony Payne helps us think biblically about church. Along with giving plenty of other practical advice, he suggests a way to walk into church that beautifully expresses what church is and why you're there—a way that every Christian can master.

If you go to church, this book is for you.

For more information or to order contact:

Matthias Media
sales@matthiasmedia.com.au
matthiasmedia.com.au

Matthias Media (USA)
sales@matthiasmedia.com
matthiasmedia.com

AVAILABLE ONLINE